CONTENTS

The erected memorial monument in Patuxent Park at the site of the Columbia Air Center in Croom, Maryland.

Acknowledgments

Before continuing, I want to honor and thank those who deserve thanks and acknowledgement for their part in the creation of this book.

First, I'd like to thank my wife Patricia Ann Ware for her love and partnership in not only everything we do, but also this book. Her encouragement and technical support to help with the writing of this book were unparalleled. I love you, my dearest.

Reggie Campbell, Chief flight instructor at Cloud Club II.

I would also like to thank Captain Reginald L. Campbell for all the hours that were spent teaching me to be an aviator, behind the controls, and during flight planning. I'll never forget the day I soloed. We had just completed a couple of circuits in the pattern at VKX airport in a Cessna 150 N9427U, and I was feeling confident. Reggie had me taxi to the end of the taxiway, he removed his seatbelt, and said to me, "Alright, one circuit in the pattern to a full stop." He then pulled the latch to the door and bumped the door open to exit the plane, he paused to turn and look back at me over his left shoulder with a smallish smile and gave me a reassuring head nod and exited the plane, and then off I went. Reggie Campbell was one of the most knowledgeable pilot instructors who has ever taught the craft. Unfortunately, Reggie has left us for the beyond. He leaves behind a legacy of aviation that is unforgettable and thousands of hours upon thousands as a pilot-in-command time, and many private pilots were made by Reggie Campbell. It was the depth of his instruction and direction during my flight training that gave me the opportunity to achieve my dreams and years later write this book.

Herbert Jones Jr., the "Godfather of Black Aviation".

Last and certainly not least was Herbert Jones Jr. I want to thank Mr. Jones for the time he invested in a life of aviation, making that dream a reality for countless numbers of people who were enamored with flying. The dividends of his investment were paid out to those of us who flew his aircraft and participated in all the aviation activities and events that he supported from the Columbia Air Center and the Cloud Club, the East Coast Chapter of the Tuskegee Airmen, and Cloud Club II. Herbert Jones Jr. was a man with a dream, and despite the circumstances, setbacks, and detours, he was determined to make that dream a reality. There may have been men wiser, but not many. Mr. Jones was a great mentor in all my days of flying. I remember the pride and happiness that showed on his face when I taxied in from my private pilot practical exam, and I had won the day, becoming his newest FAA Certified Private Pilot back in November of 2002 (certificate number 2735425). He instilled in me critical aeronautical decision making not only in flying the aircraft, but aircraft maintenance, flight planning, pilotage, and aviation weather. I remember one day, after I had received my pilot's license, I rented one of the Club's aircraft to fly a short trip to southern Maryland. It was a beautiful day outside, and I was ready; flight-plan complete, and preflight checks were done on the aircraft. I walked back inside the Cloud Club II office to finish off final preparations before activating my flight plan. Mr. Jones walked slowly over to me and said, "Did you check the weather?" I turned to him and said," Yes sir, I checked it twice this morning from the tower at Andrews AFB". He kind of nodded his head and walked away. A couple of minutes later, he came back to me and asked the exact same question in the same manner as he did the first time, "Did you check the weather?" I knew Herb Jones at this point. I had been flying under his tutelage for many years now, and something was up. So, I checked the weather again, and even though the weather was a go at W32, the area that I was flying to, 2W6, was now looking marginal for low clouds. So, I canceled the flight with much disappointment and ended up driving to that area afterwards. It was like someone waved a magic wand. I had driven about fifteen miles south, still beautiful outside, and suddenly, BAM! "Whatyah" know, "Ground Fog"! Mr. Jones was truly the Yoda of all things' aviation. I really appreciated the knowledge he shared with me as a new pilot. His investment made me more well-rounded in all things. Unfortunately, Mr. Jones is no longer with us. His best years behind him, he has joined the other Black aviation pioneers in eternity. He is loved and greatly missed. Herb was a gentle spirit. Kind of the way you would imagine Father Time to be. Herb Jones was the gate keeper to the bridge leading to the past, allowing many to see the future. His passing doesn't close the bridge but allows the bridge to remain open in our heart and in our minds. Thanks Herb, for the job well done and all that you have done for us. We all salute you.

Preface

For as far back as I can remember, I've been drawn to the sky. As a boy, I could spend hours watching aircraft trace their paths overhead, wondering where they came from and where they were going. At thirteen, I joined the Civil Air Patrol, wearing that uniform with pride and learning the basics of aeronautics while most kids my age were just starting to think about driving cars. During high school, I took ground school training, studying reciprocating engines, flight controls, weather patterns, and navigation.

In 1984, I enlisted in the U.S. Navy and completed A-School as an Aviation Support Equipment Electrician, working around the hum of engines and the smell of jet fuel. Aviation became not just a fascination, but my profession, as now I work for a large Aerospace company. Even when I wasn't in uniform, the skies were still calling out to me. After completing basic training, I began to take flying lessons at Naval Air Station Millington, Tennessee. I started there, but

I didn't complete flight training in Tennessee. I suppose I didn't feel comfortable with the instructors. I didn't think at the time that they had my best interest at heart.

In 1995, well after leaving the Naval Service, I joined the Cloud Club II, where I spent a decade learning from and standing beside a few historic African American aviators. It was there that I met Colonel Charles McGee, U.S. Air Force (Retired), one of the famed Tuskegee Airmen, whose quiet and humble demeanor never told the true story of his sacrifice and determination to be the best that he could be. My own flight instructor, former U.S. Army Captain Reginald L. Campbell, had flown helicopters for the DC National Guard. Reggie taught me precision, discipline, and courage in being an aviator. My mentor, Herbert Jones Jr., was a pioneer who had navigated the skies when the odds and discrimination were against him. "Herb," as he was known in the aviation community by his friends and his student pilots, was destined to become a key pioneer in aviation in his own right.

I'm honored to be connected and linked to a great heritage of aviation pioneers that gave their all for so many African Americans who looked to the sky and said, "I must fly". The greats in our African American aviation history, like Bessie Coleman, Eugene Bullard, John W. Greene Jr., Cornelius Coffey, Willa Beatrice Brown, and C. Alfred "Chief" Anderson, who forged a way forward at places like Columbia Air Center. I have lived near the Columbia Air Center for most of my life. For many years, I didn't know its deeply rooted significance, being one of the first African American-owned and operated airports in the United States. Columbia Air Center is more than a memorial that sits next to a corn field in Patuxent Park. It's a living bridge between the past and the present. In 2021, I married my wife Patricia at the CAC memorial site during the isolated times of Covid-19. We took our vows there in the park surrounded by history, under the same open sky that has always inspired me to fly.

This book is my tribute to those pioneers who unknowingly broke down the barriers for our sake and my invitation to future dreamers to keep moving forward towards their goals at all costs. These pages are about more than pilots and airplanes; they are about perseverance, mentorship, camaraderie, and courage to overcome stereotypes and limitations. Every takeoff is part of a connected journey, one that began centuries ago and continues to gain altitude today. So, "Let us not allow them to forget all of the struggle that has taken place". My own story is only a small portion of a much greater one. But the history that follows is not about me, it is about generations of African Americans who looked to the sky with the same determination and whose courage made flight possible for those who followed.

— Stephen Christopher Ware

Chapter 1 – The African American Experience: From the White Lion to The Civil Rights Movement

The African American story in America begins not with flight, but with forced arrival. In 1619, the English privateer White Lion brought the first recorded Africans to America, where uncertain status soon hardened into race-based chattel slavery. Over the next two centuries, the transatlantic slave trade entrenched slavery as a cornerstone of colonial and Southern economies. Despite brutal oppression, enslaved Africans preserved cultural traditions, resisted bondage, and sought freedom whenever possible. By the time of the American Revolution, African Americans were integral to the colonial population, though largely excluded from the liberty that independence promised.

The Civil War marked a turning point, transforming a fight for the Union into a struggle against slavery with the Emancipation Proclamation and the service of nearly 200,000 Black soldiers. The Union victory brought emancipation and constitutional amendments that eventually secured citizenship and voting rights. Yet Reconstruction's promise was violently suppressed, ushering in Jim Crow segregation, disenfranchisement, and racial terror. The Great Migration of the 20th century reshaped the American landscape, fueling cultural movements like the Harlem Renaissance while expanding Black political influence in urban centers. Nevertheless, systemic inequality persisted in housing, education, and employment.

World War II and its aftermath provided new momentum for change. African Americans distinguished themselves in service to their country and pressured the federal government for desegregation. The spark of Rosa Parks' arrest in 1955 and the Montgomery Bus Boycott signaled the dawn of the modern Civil Rights Movement. From the forced arrival aboard the White Lion to the organized struggle for equality, African Americans endured centuries of oppression while building a legacy of resilience, culture, and activism. From slavery to civil rights, the African American struggle for equality created the foundation upon which every aviator would later stand. Flight would become not only a new frontier of technology, but a powerful symbol of freedom itself.

This chapter lays the foundation for understanding how their pursuit of freedom and inclusion shaped both aviation history and the broader American experience.

Chapter 2 – African Americans in Aviation: Breaking the Color Barrier

Flight was barely two decades old when African Americans began their quest to enter the skies. The Wright brothers had proven human flight possible in 1903, but for Black men and women in the early 20th century, the path to the cockpit was blocked by a maze of legal, financial, and social barriers. Jim Crow laws made access to aviation schools almost impossible. Most white-owned flight schools refused Black students outright. Even those who managed to find training abroad returned to find American doors still closed. Yet, in this hostile climate, a small number of determined individuals blazed a trail.

Bessie Coleman poses for a portrait, taken circa 1926. Bessie had made plans to open a flying school before her untimely death.

Bessie Coleman (1892–1926) was a pioneering African and Native American aviator who overcame both racial and gender barriers to become the first Black woman in the world to earn a pilot's license. Born in Atlanta, Texas, to a family of sharecroppers, Coleman grew up in an era of entrenched Jim Crow segregation, with limited educational opportunities for African Americans. After moving to

Chicago in her early twenties, she became fascinated by stories of World War I pilots, but no U.S. flight school would accept her because of her race and sex. Determined to pursue her dream, she learned French and traveled to France in 1920, where she trained at the prestigious Caudron Brothers' School of Aviation. In June 1921, she received her international pilot's license from the Fédération Aéronautique Internationale, making history as a trailblazer in aviation.

Returning to the United States, Coleman became a celebrated barnstormer, performing daring aerial stunts, parachute jumps, and loop-the-loops at airshows. She used her fame to challenge racial prejudice, refusing to perform at venues that excluded African Americans, and speaking publicly about the need for Black participation in aviation. Coleman's ambition extended beyond performance as she planned to open a flight school to train future African American aviators. Her career was tragically cut short in

1926 when she died in a plane accident during a practice flight in Jacksonville, Florida. Despite her brief life, Bessie Coleman's achievements inspired generations of aviators and civil rights advocates, cementing her legacy as a symbol of courage, determination, and the unyielding pursuit of equality.

Although Eugene Bullard was not the only Black combat pilot to fly in World War I, he was the only African American who participated in aerial combat. The slogan on the side of his fighter plane read, "All Blood Runs Red".

Eugene Bullard (1895–1961) was an African American who became America's first Black military pilot, earning distinction as a combat aviator in France during World War I. Born in Columbus, Georgia, Bullard grew up amid the harsh realities of Jim Crow segregation and racial violence. Determined to escape these conditions, he left home as a teenager and traveled abroad, eventually settling in France, where he found greater social acceptance. When World War I broke out, Bullard joined the French Foreign Legion and later served in the 170th Infantry Regiment, earning the Croix de Guerre for bravery in combat. In 1917, he trained as a pilot and flew combat missions with the French Air Service, becoming a symbol of courage and skill.

After the war, Bullard remained in France, working as a nightclub owner, drummer, and cultural figure in Paris during the Jazz Age, befriending artists and writers such as Louis Armstrong, Josephine Baker, and Ernest Hemingway. He served again during World War II as part of the French

Resistance, aiding in the fight against Nazi occupation. Forced to flee after France fell in 1940, Bullard returned to the United States, where, despite his extraordinary record, he lived in relative obscurity and worked modest jobs. He received little recognition from his home country during his lifetime, but in 1959, France honored him as a Knight of the Légion d'Honneur. Today, Eugene Bullard is remembered as a trailblazer who broke racial barriers in aviation and served with valor in two world wars, embodying the complex intersection of race, patriotism, and perseverance.

William J. Powell, in his book "Black Wings," in a segregated America in 1934, urged America's Black youth to "Fill the Skies with Black Wings".

William J. Powell (1897–1942) was an African American aviator, entrepreneur, and advocate whose mission was to open the skies to Black Americans. Born in Kentucky and raised in Chicago, Powell served in the U.S. Army during World War I as part of an engineering battalion in France. After the war, he earned a degree in engineering from the University of Illinois. Inspired by the possibilities of aviation but excluded from flight training programs in the United States due to racial discrimination, Powell eventually found a school in Los Angeles willing to train him. By the late 1920s, he had earned his pilot's license and turned his attention to promoting aviation as a field for African Americans, seeing it as a path to economic empowerment and racial advancement.

In 1929, Powell founded the Bessie Coleman Aero Club in Los Angeles, named in honor of the pioneering Black woman pilot who had inspired him. Through the club, he organized flight instruction, airshows, and public events aimed at sparking interest in aviation among African Americans. He also wrote Black Wings (1934), a book that combined autobiography with a passionate call for Black participation in aviation, arguing that mastery of flight could inspire pride, opportunity, and progress in the African American community. Powell's tireless work helped lay the groundwork for the inclusion of Black pilots in the military and the growth of African American aviation organizations. Though his life was cut short by illness in 1942, William J.

Powell is remembered as a visionary who blended technical skills, entrepreneurial spirit, and activism to challenge the racial barriers of his time. Coleman, Bullard, and Powell did not fly to be remembered as icons. They flew because the sky called them, and in answering that call, they carved a path that history could not ignore.

Together, the lives of Bessie Coleman, Eugene Bullard, and William J. Powell illuminate both the extraordinary barriers African Americans faced in aviation and the remarkable determination with which they broke through them. Coleman, denied training in the United States, journeyed abroad to become the first Black woman licensed pilot, using her fame to inspire others and challenge segregation. Bullard, fleeing Jim Crow America, rose to distinction as the first Black American combat aviator in France, later embodying resilience as a soldier, entertainer, and resistance fighter. Powell, building on the legacy of pioneers like Coleman, worked tirelessly to create opportunities for

African Americans in aviation, founding institutions, and writing Black Wings to promote both pride and progress. Though each encountered racism and exclusion in their homeland, they forged paths that redefined what was possible for African Americans in the air. Their legacies not only expanded the story of aviation but also stand as enduring testaments to courage, vision, and the pursuit of equality.

John W. Greene Jr. takes a picture in front of an Aeronca Champ. Greene was a committed master as a pilot, aircraft mechanic, and flight instructor.

Chapter 3 – John W. Greene Jr.: Mentor, Educator, Pioneer

By the late 1930s, African American aviators had proven their skills in the air. Bessie Coleman had inspired a generation, Eugene Bullard had flown in combat, and William J. Powell had laid the groundwork for building a Black aviation community. But the next leap forward would not be measured in solo flights. It would be measured in classrooms and training fields, where young men and women learned to master the craft of flying. One of the most important figures in this transition from inspiration to institution was John W. Greene Jr (1901- 1988).

John W. Greene Jr. was born in Chattanooga, Tennessee, on Christmas Day in the year 1901. Later in his younger life, he moved with his family to Elberton, Georgia. His educational pursuits took him from there to the Hampton Institute (now Hampton University) in the 1920s. It was during his time at Hampton that Greene's fascination with aviation began. One day, on his way to work at a local shipyard where he was employed as a Shipfitter's apprentice, Greene witnessed an airplane crash. It could be said that this unfortunate accident sparked his interest in aviation. It was then that Greene temporarily discontinued his quest for higher education and moved to Massachusetts, where in 1922 he took his first airplane ride for a dollar and shortly afterwards, began taking flying lessons. These were the experiences early in John's life that solidified his commitment to aviation.

Greene earned his private pilot's license in 1929 (certificate number 10658) at Denison Airport, followed by a commercial license at East Bay Airport by 1932. In the same year he received a "Transport Pilot" rating (today's Airline Transport Pilot License). At some time during the first few years of the 1930s Greene received his Flight Instructor's and Ground School Instructor's licenses. He also received an aircraft and engine mechanic's certificate by the end of 1932. John W. Greene held both a pilot license with advanced ratings and an aircraft and engine mechanics license, distinguishing him as the first African American hold both at the same time.

In 1940, Greene relocated to Washington, D.C., to organize and teach an aviation mechanics program at Phelps Vocational High School. Around the same time, he co-founded the Cloud Club. The Cloud Club was an aviation club for Black pilots. Initially based at Beacon Field in Alexandria, Virginia, the group faced racial exclusion and regulatory obstacles, which compelled Greene and his fellow aviators to seek a field of their own.

After encountering discrimination at Beacon Field. Greene and fellow Cloud Club members leased a 450-acre farm near the Patuxent River in Croom, Maryland, paying $30 monthly. They built an airfield that opened in 1941 as Riverside Field, later renamed Columbia Air Center around 1944–45. Under Greene's leadership as co-owner and manager, the center became the first Black-owned-and-operated licensed airport in Maryland and among the first in the nation.

Columbia Air Center was more than an airfield; it was an educational hub. The facility included multiple turf runways, hangars, classrooms, a fleet of aircraft, and it hosted a Civil Air Patrol cadet squadron. This was the first African American Civil Air Patrol squadron on the East Coast. Columbia Air Center offered flight lessons, ground school sessions, mechanics training, charter services, and community events such as air shows and races. Greene highly emphasized aviation education for youth. Many of whom would become pilots and mechanics because of this center. Columbia Air Center operated under Greene's management until his 1954 retirement; the airport closed in 1956 after lease issues, declining aviation interest, and the beginnings of integregation.

John W. Greene Jr.'s life exemplifies how vision, technical expertise, and unwavering determination can transform personal passion into a broader movement for empowerment. From mastering dual certifications in aviation and mechanics to founding a pioneering aviation school and airfield, Greene shattered barriers that had long excluded African Americans from the skies. His efforts at Columbia Air Center fostered a generation of aspiring pilots and mechanics and affirmed aviation as accessible to Black communities. John W. Greene Jr. turned passion into education, creating institutions that ensured aviation was not just for the few but for the many. His legacy lives on in every African American student who dared to dream of the cockpit.

Cornileus Coffey was a self-taught pilot in the 1920s before earning his pilot's license in the 1930s and became the first Black licensed Aircraft Engine Mechanic in the country.

Chapter 4 – Cornelius Coffey: Aviator, Educator, Entrepreneur

Cornelius Coffey (1903–1994) was a pioneering African American aviator, mechanic, and educator whose career opened pathways for Black participation in aviation. Born in Newport, Arkansas, Coffey developed an interest in mechanics at an early age. He initially pursued work as an auto mechanic, but his fascination with flight grew during the 1920s when aviation captured national attention following Charles Lindbergh's transatlantic flight. Despite a widespread belief that African Americans lacked a place in aviation, Coffey resolved to pursue his dream. This determination marked the beginning of a career that would overcome systemic barriers in both flight training and aviation mechanics.

Like many African Americans of his time, Coffey encountered discrimination when attempting to enroll in flight schools. Refused entry because of his race, he partnered with fellow Black aviation enthusiast John C. Robinson to form a study group, reading aeronautical engineering manuals and taking mechanics classes where possible. Eventually, Coffey and Robinson managed to secure training at the Curtiss-Wright School of Aviation in Chicago in the early 1930s. When Black students were denied classroom participation, they persevered by learning through observation and practice, excelling in both theory and skill. Their persistence earned Coffey his mechanic's license in 1931 and his pilot's license in 1932, establishing him as one of the earliest licensed African American aviators and the first licensed Black aircraft mechanic in the United States.

Recognizing that opportunity for African Americans in aviation required institutional support, Coffey helped establish the Challenger Air Pilots Association in Chicago. In 1938, he co-founded the Coffey School of Aeronautics at Robbins, Illinois, one of the first Black-owned and operated flight schools in the nation. The school provided flight and mechanics training for African Americans who were otherwise excluded from white-run aviation programs. The Coffey School became a vital center for aviation education in the Black community, nurturing a generation of pilots and technicians who would play significant roles during World War II and beyond.

During World War II, Coffey's school was selected to participate in the Civilian Pilot Training Program (CPTP), a government initiative designed to expand the pool of trained pilots. Through this program, many of Coffey's students went on to become members of the famed Tuskegee Airmen, the all-Black United States Army Air Force Fighter Group that proved essential to Allied air operations and helped challenge racist assumptions about African American abilities in aviation. Coffey's role as a teacher and mentor meant that he indirectly contributed to one of the most celebrated chapters in American military aviation history.

After the war, Coffey continued his work in aviation, training new pilots and advocating for African American inclusion in the rapidly growing field of commercial and private aviation. Though he did not achieve the national fame of figures like Bessie Coleman or the Tuskegee Airmen, his influence as an educator, institution builder, and barrier-breaker was profound. Cornelius Coffey proved that education and opportunity could lift a community as surely as wings lift a plane. His school prepared not just pilots, but a movement that would soar far beyond Robbins, Illinois.

While Willa Beatrice Brown was chasing her dreams in aviation, she ran a sandwich shop at Harlem airfield that fostered connections between aviators, mechanics and instructors that fueled her groundbreaking charge in aviation, education, and Civil Rights.

Chapter 5 – Willa Beatrice Brown: Aviator, Educator, Public Servant, Civil Rights Advocate

Willa Beatrice Brown (1906–1992) was a pioneering aviator, educator, and civil rights advocate whose life reshaped the trajectory of Black aviation in America. Born in Glasgow, Kentucky, she pursued higher education with determination, earning degrees from Indiana State Teachers College and Northwestern University. Inspired by Bessie Coleman's legacy, Brown enrolled in flight training at Chicago's segregated Harlem Field, where she earned her private pilot's license in 1937 and becoming the first African American woman in the United States to do so. Her passion for aviation was matched by her technical acumen; she later earned a Master Mechanic's certificate and a commercial pilot's license, breaking barriers in both flight and aircraft maintenance.

Brown's impact extended far beyond her personal achievements. In 1938, she co-founded the Coffey School of Aeronautics with her future husband, Cornelius Coffey. This institution became the first Black-owned and operated flight school in the country and trained hundreds of African American pilots, many of whom would go on to serve as Tuskegee Airmen during World War II. Brown also became the first Black officer in the Civil Air Patrol, using her position to advocate for the inclusion of African Americans in the Civilian Pilot Training Program. Her lobbying efforts with Congress and the War Department were instrumental in opening military aviation to Black pilots.

In addition to her aviation work, Brown was deeply committed to education and public service. She taught aviation mechanics and ground school in Chicago's public schools, mentoring young students and encouraging them to pursue careers in aviation and engineering. In the 1940s, she made history again by becoming the first African American woman to run for Congress, campaigning on a platform of racial equality, education reform, and economic opportunity. Though she did not win, her candidacy marked a significant moment in the political empowerment of Black women.

Brown's legacy continued through her service on the Federal Aviation Administration's Women's Advisory Committee, where she worked to expand opportunities for women in aviation. She remained active in civic life until her retirement in 1971, always championing the causes of education, equity, and innovation. Her contributions were recognized posthumously with numerous honors, and her story remains a cornerstone of African American aviation history.

Willa Beatrice Brown's life was a testament to perseverance, vision, and leadership. She not only soared through the skies but also dismantled the barriers that kept others grounded. Her work laid the foundation for generations of aviators, educators, and activists, proving that flight is not just a matter of altitude, but of attitude, access, and audacity.

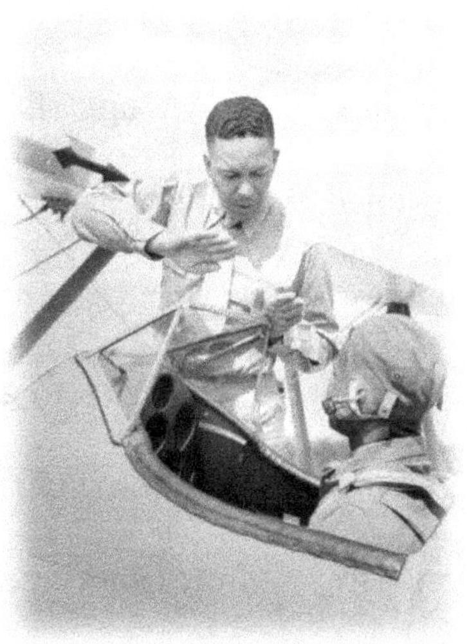

Charles Alfred "Chief" Anderson was largely responsible for the successful training of the famed combat pilots; the Tuskegee Airmen.

Chapter 6 – C. Alfred "Chief" Anderson: "The Father of Black Aviation"

Charles Alfred "Chief" Anderson (1907–1996) earned his place in history as the "Father of Black Aviation" and the lead flight instructor of the Tuskegee Airmen. Born in Bryn Mawr, Pennsylvania, Anderson developed an early fascination with airplanes at a time when African Americans were almost entirely excluded from aviation. Rebuffed by every formal flight school he approached because of his race, he nevertheless refused to give up. He taught himself aviation theory, studied aircraft mechanics, and sought out informal opportunities to fly. After years of persistence, he finally convinced aviator Russell Thaw to give him lessons in 1929. By 1932, Anderson had earned his pilot's license, becoming the first African American to receive a transport pilot's certificate, an advanced rating that made him a highly qualified pilot.

Anderson's early career was marked by both teaching and performing aerial demonstrations. He became a respected pilot within the small but growing African American aviation community, working alongside pioneers such as John C. Robinson and Cornelius Coffey. His expertise in both piloting and mechanics earned him the nickname "Chief," reflecting the esteem in which he was held by his peers. Anderson also became known for his airshows and barnstorming flights, which inspired young Black men and women to see aviation as a possible career despite systemic barriers. His reputation as both a skilled aviator and a capable teacher laid the foundation for his most enduring contribution, training the Tuskegee Airmen.

In 1940, Tuskegee Institute in Alabama launched an aviation program under the newly created Civilian Pilot Training Program (CPTP), and Anderson was hired as its chief instructor. His role was transformative: he not only taught African American students how to fly, but he also helped prove to skeptical military officials that Black pilots could succeed at the highest levels of aviation. In 1941, Anderson famously took First Lady Eleanor Roosevelt on a flight over Tuskegee, an event that drew national attention. When she landed, Roosevelt declared with conviction that “Negroes can fly,” a statement that bolstered support for the continued training of African American pilots and directly influenced the establishment of the Tuskegee Airmen program.

As chief flight instructor, Anderson trained hundreds of African American pilots during World War II. Many of these men went on to serve in the 99th Fighter Squadron and the 332nd Fighter Group, better known as the Tuskegee Airmen. Under Anderson's leadership, these pilots received the rigorous training necessary to succeed in combat, where they ultimately distinguished themselves as one of the most respected combat units of the war. Anderson's ability to combine technical skill with patience and mentorship ensured that his students were prepared not only as pilots but also as leaders, proving the falsity of racist assumptions about African American capability.

C. Alfred "Chief" Anderson's life stands as a testament to perseverance, skill, and the transformative power of education in breaking racial barriers. From a young man who taught himself the principles of flight when no school would admit him, he rose to become the first African American transport-rated pilot and the chief instructor of the Tuskegee

Airmen, whose wartime success reshaped the American military and social history. His mentorship not only produced some of the most accomplished pilots of World War II but also helped dismantle entrenched prejudices about African American abilities in aviation. Beyond the war, Anderson remained a tireless advocate for Black participation in flight, ensuring that opportunities he once fought to create would expand for future generations. His legacy endures as both a symbol of determination against adversity and as a cornerstone in the story of African American achievement in aviation. Chief Anderson's legacy is more than his own flight hours. It is the hundreds of pilots he trained, the stereotypes he shattered, and the nation he forced to see that African Americans could be skilled and effective combat pilots in US military service.

Captain Andrew D. "Jug" Turner, second from the right, the CO of the 100th FS, with several of his pilots posing for a picture next to his mount, the North American P-51C Mustang called Skipper's Darling III.

Chapter 7 – The Tuskegee Airmen: Achievers, Warriors, Pride of the African American Aviation Experience

The Tuskegee Airmen were the first African American military pilots in U.S. history, trained at Tuskegee Institute in Alabama during World War II. Their formation was a direct result of years of pressure from civil rights organizations and Black leaders, who pushed for African Americans to be included in the U.S. Army Air Corps. The program began in 1941 under the Civilian Pilot Training Program, with Tuskegee selected as the training site due to its established aeronautical program and the leadership of Chief Flight Instructor C. Alfred "Chief" Anderson. Despite skepticism and open hostility from segments of the military establishment, the program produced a cadre of highly skilled fighter and bomber pilots, navigators, mechanics, and support personnel, disproving racist assumptions about African American abilities in aviation.

The first unit of Tuskegee pilots, the 99th Fighter Squadron, deployed to North Africa in 1943 under the command of Captain Benjamin O. Davis Jr. Initially flying P-40 Warhawks, they carried out ground attack missions against Axis forces. Although subjected to criticism from some white commanders who doubted their effectiveness, the 99th soon demonstrated its skill in combat, supporting Allied advances in North Africa, Sicily, and Italy. Their persistence and professionalism set the stage for the expansion of Tuskegee-trained units into larger groups.

Colonel Benjiman O. Davis Jr., the OIC of the 332nd FG. In a briefing with his officers at Ramitelli, Italy.

In 1944, the 332nd Fighter Group was activated, combining the 99th with three additional squadrons—the 100th, 301st, and 302nd. Flying P-47 Thunderbolts and later P-51 Mustangs, the group was based at Ramitelli, Italy, and assigned long-range bomber escort duties. Their aircraft, famously painted with red tails, earned them the nickname "Red Tails." They escorted heavy bombers such as the B-17 Flying Fortress and B-24 Liberator on missions deep into Germany and occupied Europe, ensuring their charges reached targets with minimal losses.

The 332nd flew over 15,000 combat sorties and completed more than 1,500 missions between 1943 and 1945. They destroyed more than 260 enemy aircraft in air-to-air combat and nearly 1,000 more on the ground. The group sank a German destroyer in the harbor of Trieste, Italy, a rare feat for fighter aircraft, and earned a Distinguished Unit Citation for its performance escorting bombers to Berlin on March 24, 1945. Their pilots became known for disciplined flying, and bomber crews frequently requested "Red Tail" escorts because of their reputation for protection. Among their notable achievements, Tuskegee pilots shot down advanced German aircraft such as the Me 262 jet fighter, proving their capability against the Luftwaffe's most modern weapons.

At the center of the Tuskegee Airmen's success was Colonel Benjamin O. Davis Jr., who commanded both the 99th Fighter Squadron and later the 332nd Fighter Group. The son of the U.S. Army's first Black general, Davis embodied discipline and excellence. A 1936 graduate of West Point, where he endured four years of isolation from his white classmates, Davis carried the same resilience into his military leadership. Under his command, the Tuskegee Airmen excelled despite systemic prejudice, and Davis himself went on to a distinguished Air Force career, eventually becoming the first African American general in the U.S. Air Force. His leadership provided the foundation upon which the Tuskegee Airmen earned their legacy. The Tuskegee Airmen carried more than bombs and bullets; they carried the hopes of a people. In their valor, they earned victory both in the skies of Europe and in the fight for dignity at home.

Colonel Charles McGee, a Tuskegee Airman and part of the famed 332nd FG, is noted as having flown combat missions during three U.S. wars. He holds the record for the most combat missions flown by any U.S. Combat pilot in U.S. military history.

Charles E. McGee (1919–2022) was one of the most celebrated Tuskegee Airmen, whose career spanned three wars. Born in Cleveland, Ohio, McGee joined the Army in 1942 and trained at Tuskegee, graduating as a pilot in 1943. Assigned to the 302nd Fighter Squadron of the 332nd Fighter Group, McGee flew his first combat missions from bases in Italy. In World War II alone, he flew 137 combat missions, escorting bombers and attacking ground targets across Europe.

After World War II, McGee remained in the military, building one of the longest flying careers in U.S. Air Force history. He flew combat missions in both the Korean War and the Vietnam War, ultimately completing an astounding 409 combat missions across the three conflicts. Rising to the rank of colonel, McGee held command positions and became a role model for younger generations of pilots. His service record of over 6,000 flight hours in fighters alone made him one of the most accomplished aviators in U.S. history.

In later life, McGee became an ambassador for the Tuskegee Airmen, speaking widely about the group's history and their fight against prejudice. He was awarded the Congressional Gold Medal in 2007 along with his fellow Tuskegee Airmen and continued to receive recognition for his extraordinary service, including an honorary promotion to brigadier general in 2020 at the age of 100. McGee's story not only reflects personal achievement but also the broader struggle and triumph of African American pilots who proved their worth through unmatched dedication and courage.

The Tuskegee Airmen's story is one of resilience, excellence, and transformation. In the face of institutional racism, they built a combat record that rivaled or surpassed that of any unit in the U.S. Army Air Forces, protecting bombers, destroying enemy aircraft, and earning respect through discipline and valor. Leaders like Benjamin O. Davis Jr. provided the vision and structure, while individuals such as Charles E. McGee embodied the lasting impact of their contributions across decades of service. Their achievements helped pave the way for the desegregation of the U.S. military in 1948 and stand as a landmark in both African American and aviation history. The legacy of the Tuskegee Airmen endures not only in their wartime record but in their role as pioneers of equality in America's armed forces.

The Columbia Air Center's aircraft hangar hosted many services for aviation, including aircraft maintenance, ground school training, and pilot training.

Chapter 8 - The Columbia Air Center – The Genesis of the African American Aviation Community

The Columbia Air Center, located in Croom, Maryland, was one of the first Black-owned and-operated airports in the United States and a pioneering institution in African American aviation history. Established in 1941, the center was founded by a group of Black aviators led by John W.

Greene Jr. and members of the Cloud Club, an aviation organization formed to provide opportunities for African Americans excluded from white-controlled airfields. Built on leased farmland near the Patuxent River, the Columbia Air Center represented both a practical and symbolic response to systemic racism in aviation—creating a safe space where African Americans could fly, train, and gather without restriction.

The Cloud Club played a crucial role in the creation and management of the Columbia Air Center. Founded by Black pilots who were denied access to facilities at airports like Beacon Field in Virginia, the Cloud Club organized lessons, meetings, and advocacy for African American participation in aviation. Its members saw aviation not only as a technical skill but as a vehicle for racial uplift and progress. By pooling resources and community support, they transformed their dream into a tangible institution, one that directly challenged segregationist barriers.

The Columbia Air Center grew to encompass multiple turf runways, hangars, classrooms, and support buildings. Its services went beyond recreational flying—it offered flight instruction, ground school, and mechanic training programs that prepared young African Americans for professional roles in aviation. Charter flights, aircraft rentals, and community events such as air shows and races broadened its scope. The center also hosted a Civil Air Patrol squadron, which gave Black youth their first structured opportunities in aviation during World War II, further embedding the institution in both local and national aviation networks. The Columbia Air Center was more than an airfield; it was a declaration of self-determination. Though its runways have long since grown quiet, its spirit continues to guide the communities that built it.

Members of the Columbia Air Center's "Cloud Club" standing in front of the club's former USAAF trainer, a Vultee Valiant BT-13.

The success of the Columbia Air Center was deeply rooted in the local African American community, which rallied behind the project. Churches, civic organizations, and Black-owned businesses provided financial and moral support, while families encouraged their children to participate in their programs. Community air shows drew crowds across Prince George's County and beyond, turning the airfield into both an educational and social hub. The center symbolized progress at a time when African Americans were still barred from many mainstream institutions and professional pathways.

For African American aviators, the Columbia Air Center provided an indispensable training ground. Many pilots earned their licenses at the field, while others honed their skills to prepare for advanced opportunities in military and commercial aviation. The school's emphasis on mechanics and engineering complemented its pilot training, producing a cadre of technicians and ground crew members as well. At a time when Black aviators were virtually invisible in commercial airlines and military leadership, the Columbia Air Center carved out a vital space for technical education and professional development.

Herbert Jones Jr., Tuskegee Airman, majority owner and operator of the first African American airline, and President and owner of Cloud Club II.

Herbert Jones Jr. (1923 - 2020) was among the many aviators associated with the Columbia Air Center and was a dedicated pilot who trained and flew there during its peak years. Jones, a former Tuskegee Airmen, became an accomplished flight instructor, contributing to the center's mission of producing skilled Black aviators. He also played a role in connecting the field to broader aviation networks, participating in events and educational initiatives that drew attention to the capabilities of African American pilots. Jones also used his skills as an instructor pilot to teach youth, associated with the Columbia Cadet Squadron of Civil Air Patrol. He taught cadets the principles of aviation and aerospace education. Jones's aviation skills and background also led him to become a Search and Rescue pilot for the National Capital Wing of CAP. Later in his CAP flying career as a Lt. Colonel, he became the National Capital Wing's Search and Rescue coordinator.

In 1972, Jones as a member of an all-black organization of pilots and businessmen established the IAA, The International Air Association. This was the first Black-owned airline to be established in the continental United States. The organization purchased a 100 seat Douglas DC-7 Passenger aircraft and establishing charter service to locations such as The Bahamas and Trinadad, New York, Houston, and Miami. As IAA experienced tough economic times, the Airline and the business declined and eventually closed.

Herb Jones continued in the mindset of an aviator and instructor and in 1987 he opened a Flight School of his own called Cloud Club II. The Flight School trained over 200 pilots in primary flight training. Many went on to jobs in commercial, military, and federal aviation. Just as John W. Greene had done decades earlier, Jones kept alive the original embodiment of the Columbia Air Center and Cloud Club for another generation that looked to the skies to fulfill a dream and desire to fly. Where exclusion and discrimination challenged the dreams and aspirations of many African American, there were those like Herbert Jones Jr. who would not allow those dreams to fade and die. Herbert Jones Jr.'s career spanned more than thirty years. Thirty years of dedication to the principles of flying, progress, and prosperity. Herb Jones ends his career as a highly celebrated figure in the Black Aviation community.

His career exemplified the generation of aviators whose opportunities were made possible by institutions like Columbia Air Center.

Despite its successes, the Columbia Air Center faced challenges after World War II. The growing integration of the U.S. military and commercial aviation in the late 1940s and early 1950s began to draw aspiring Black aviators to new opportunities elsewhere. Economic pressures and leasing issues compounded the difficulties, and the center ultimately closed in 1956. Yet even in its decline, its historical significance as one of the earliest Black-operated airfields remained clear, and its alumni continued to influence aviation and engineering professions nationwide.

The Columbia Air Center's legacy lies in its role as a pioneer of inclusion, education, and community empowerment in aviation. It nurtured pilots, instructors, and mechanics who would go on to serve in the military, enter professional aviation, and inspire new generations. Just as important, it demonstrated the power of African American self-determination in overcoming segregation, proving that excellence could flourish when communities created their own institutions. The Columbia Air Center stands as a precursor to the eventual integration of African Americans into all areas of modern aviation, military, commercial, and private. The Columbia Air Center left behind a legacy of courage, vision, and progress that reshaped the possibilities of flight for future generations.

Guion Bluford, noted for being the first African American to fly into space, circa 1983.

Chapter 9 – African Americans in Modern Aviation: Civilian, Military, and Space

The future of African Americans in commercial aviation continues to expand, as representation within major airlines steadily grows. Once excluded from airline cockpits and management, Black pilots, flight attendants, and executives now occupy positions of influence and responsibility. Organizations such as the Organization of Black Aerospace

Professionals (OBAP) and the Tuskegee Airmen, Inc. play a vital role in providing scholarships, mentorship, and advocacy to ensure the pipeline of African American talent remains strong. As airlines face increasing pilot shortages, opportunities are opening for African Americans to enter not only as pilots but also as aviation managers, engineers, and safety experts, bringing diversity to a field that thrives on global connectivity.

In aerospace, African Americans are making significant strides as engineers, designers, and innovators in cutting-edge fields such as unmanned aerial systems (drones), sustainable aviation fuels, and advanced aircraft design. Companies like Boeing, Lockheed Martin, Northrop Grumman and Raytheon now actively recruit diverse talent, while historically Black colleges and universities (HBCUs) strengthen engineering and aviation programs to prepare students for aerospace careers. With the growth of electric aircraft and emerging technologies, African Americans are positioned to contribute to the industry's transformation, shaping the next generation of flight systems and setting new standards in innovation.

African Americans continue to build upon the legacy of the Tuskegee Airmen by excelling in military aviation. Today, Black pilots fly some of the most advanced aircraft in the world, including the F-35 fighter jet and C-17 Globemaster III transport aircraft. Leadership roles have also expanded, with African Americans reaching higher ranks in the Air Force, Navy, Marines, and Army aviation branches. The military's focus on diversity and inclusion ensures that African Americans not only contribute as aviators but also as commanders, strategists, and trainers, paving the way for more representation in decision-making roles.

George London is one of 29 Black pilots to complete the rigorous USAF Test Pilot School, making him one of the smartest and most skilled aviators on the planet.

Lt. Colonel George G. London Jr. carved a groundbreaking path through the U.S. Air Force as one of its first Black test pilots, defying racial barriers and technical challenges with quiet tenacity. Enlisting in 1965 during the height of the Civil Rights Movement, London later graduated at the top of his class from North Carolina A&T State University with a degree in mechanical engineering. In 1973, he entered pilot training at Webb Air Force Base, where he not only earned his wings but stayed on as a T-38 instructor. His career reached historic heights when he became the first African

American test pilot of the Boeing C-17 Globemaster III, one of the largest and most complex aircraft in the Air Force fleet. He was also one of only 29 Black graduates in the 75-year history of the elite Air Force Test Pilot School, a distinction that placed him among the most technically skilled aviators in military history.

After retiring from active duty, London transitioned into a second career that was equally impactful: education and mentorship. For 17 years, he taught physics at Bishop McNamara High School in Forestville, Maryland, earning a reputation as a brilliant and compassionate educator who made science accessible to young minds. But his commitment to aviation never waned. He founded a flight school in Fort Washington, Maryland, named for the "Godfather of Black Aviation", H.J Aviation, where he continues to teach young Black students how to fly, using his own story as a living example of perseverance and excellence. His legacy bridges military achievement and community empowerment, proving that the cockpit is not just a place of flight, it's a platform for transformation.

Guion Bluford is an extremely accomplished pilot having logged over 5,200 hours of jet flight time alone.

Colonel Guion S. Bluford Jr. launched into history as the first African American astronaut to travel into space, but his journey began in the cockpit of a fighter jet. After earning a degree in aerospace engineering from Penn State in 1964, Bluford joined the U.S. Air Force and earned his pilot wings in 1966. He flew 144 combat missions during the Vietnam War, including 65 over North Vietnam, as a member of the 557th Tactical Fighter Squadron. Following his tour, he served as a flight instructor and later earned both a master's and Ph.D. in aerospace engineering from the Air Force Institute of Technology. In 1978, while finishing his dissertation, Bluford was selected from over 10,000 applicants to join NASA's astronaut corps. He flew four Space Shuttle missions between 1983 and 1992, logging over 688 hours in space aboard Challenger, Discovery, and Atlantis, and contributed to scientific research and satellite deployment.

After retiring from active duty in 1993, Bluford transitioned into leadership roles in the aerospace industry and public service. He earned an MBA from the University of Houston at Clear Lake and became vice president and general manager of the Aerospace Sector at Federal Data Corporation in Maryland. He later served on numerous boards, including the National Space Club, the U.S. Space Foundation, and the Aerospace Corporation, helping shape policy and education in space science. Bluford was inducted into the International Space Hall of Fame in 1997 and remains a powerful advocate for STEM education and minority representation in aerospace. His post-military career reflects a lifelong commitment to innovation, mentorship, and expanding the boundaries of possibility.

The inclusion of African Americans in space exploration represents one of the most profound achievements in aviation history. From pioneers like Guion Bluford, the first African American in space, to NASA astronauts such as Victor Glover, who recently served aboard the International Space Station, the role of African Americans in shaping spaceflight continues to grow. The Artemis program, aimed at returning humans to the Moon and preparing for missions to Mars, is creating opportunities for African American astronauts, engineers, and mission specialists to take part in humanity's next giant leap. Private space companies such as SpaceX and Blue Origin further widen the horizon for African American talent in the commercial spaceflight sector.

Ensuring the future of African Americans in aviation and aerospace requires strong educational and mentorship pipelines. Programs at HBCUs, youth aviation camps, and STEM outreach initiatives are already inspiring the next generation of aviators and engineers. Flight schools and partnerships with organizations like OBAP and the Experimental Aircraft Association (EAA) provide hands-on training, ensuring that African American students are equipped not only with technical skills but also with the confidence to pursue careers in flight. By investing in these programs, communities help secure a future where diversity in aviation is not an exception but the norm.

The future also involves African Americans in aviation stepping into global leadership roles, influencing policy, sustainability, and innovation in a rapidly evolving industry. As climate change reshapes aviation priorities, African American leaders and researchers can shape sustainable practices in fuel, aircraft design, and air traffic systems. Beyond the cockpit and laboratories, representation in government agencies such as the Federal Aviation Administration (FAA) and the Department of Defense ensures African American voices influence regulation, safety, and international collaboration.

Gen. "CQ" Brown Jr. has totaled an impressive 3,100 hours of flight time in 20 fixed and rotary wing aircraft. The General was also a former instructor at "Red Flag".

General Charles Q. Brown Jr. made history as a trailblazing leader in the United States Air Force, culminating in his appointment as the 21st Chairman of the Joint Chiefs of Staff, the nation's highest-ranking military officer from 2023 to 2025. Commissioned in 1984 through the ROTC program at Texas Tech University, Brown rose through the ranks as a decorated fighter pilot with over 3,100 flight hours, including 130 combat hours primarily in the F-16. His command portfolio spanned elite units such as the U.S. Air Force Weapons School, the 8th and 31st Fighter Wings, and major theater commands including U.S. Air Forces Central Command and Pacific Air Forces. Brown's leadership was instrumental during operations like Enduring Freedom, Odyssey Dawn, and Inherent Resolve, and he became the first African American to lead a branch of the U.S. Armed

Forces when appointed Chief of Staff of the Air Force in 2020.

Following his retirement in 2025, Brown transitioned into academia and public service, accepting a two-year appointment as Executive-in-Residence at Duke University. There, he joined both the Sanford School of Public Policy and the Pratt School of Engineering, contributing to interdisciplinary programs focused on national security, ethics, and leadership. Brown co-teaches courses in American Grand Strategy and helps shape Duke's Character Forward initiative, which integrates moral reasoning into technical education. His post-military career reflects a continued commitment to mentorship and civic engagement, using his decades of strategic experience to inspire the next generation of public servants and defense leaders.

From commercial airlines to aerospace innovation, from military aviation to the frontiers of space, the future of African Americans in aviation is both promising and expansive. The groundwork laid by pioneers such as Bessie Coleman, Eugene Bullard, and the Tuskegee Airmen has created a legacy of resilience and excellence that continues to inspire new generations. As opportunities broaden through education, mentorship, and global demand for skilled aviators and engineers, African Americans are poised not only to participate in aviation's next chapter but also to lead it. Their growing presence across every sector ensures that the skies and beyond will increasingly reflect the diversity, creativity, and strength of the entire nation.

Barrington Irving standing on the wing of "Inspiration". Irving a master of resourcefulness and persuasion, approached aerospace and aircraft manufactures to donate parts and components to build and fly the inspiration around the world.

Chapter 10 – An African American Aviation Pioneer of Today, Barrington Irving: Explorer, Entrepreneur, Educator

Barrington Irving's career is a testament to vision, grit, and the transformative power of aviation. Born in Kingston, Jamaica in 1983 and raised in Miami, Florida, Irving was initially drawn to football and received multiple scholarship offers. But a chance encounter with a United Airlines pilot at age 15 changed his trajectory. That pilot invited him into a cockpit, sparking a lifelong passion for flight. Irving turned down athletic scholarships and pursued aviation instead, eventually earning his private, commercial, and certified flight instructor licenses while studying aerospace science at Florida Memorial University.

In 2007, at just 23 years old, Irving made history by becoming the youngest person and the first Black pilot to fly solo around the world. His aircraft, a Columbia 400 named Inspiration, was built from over $300,000 in donated parts. The 24,600-mile journey spanned four continents and 27 countries, earning him a place in the Guinness Book of World Records. But Irving didn't just fly for fame, he flew to inspire. His mission was to show young people, especially those from underserved communities, that they could achieve greatness through STEM and aviation.

Following his historic flight, Irving founded Experience Aviation, a nonprofit dedicated to hands-on STEM education. Through this organization, he launched programs that brought students into hangars and classrooms, teaching them to build aircraft, solve engineering challenges, and explore real-world science. In 2014, he expanded his reach with The Flying Classroom, a global digital curriculum that blends expedition-based learning with STEM instruction. Students follow Irving's travels to places like the Amazon, the Sahara, and the Arctic, connecting adventure with academic rigor.

Irving's work has earned him widespread recognition, including honors from the U.S. Congress and the Jamaican government. He's been named a National Geographic Emerging Explorer and featured in numerous educational and aviation publications. Yet his focus remains on empowering youth. He continues to mentor students, speak at schools, and advocate for diversity in aviation and STEM fields. His programs have reached thousands of learners across the U.S. and beyond, helping to close opportunity gaps and ignite curiosity.

Barrington Irving's career is far more than a flight path, it's a blueprint for impact. From cockpit to classroom, he has redefined what it means to be a pilot in the modern age. His legacy is not just in the miles he's flown, but in the minds he's lifted. For writers, educators, and historians alike, Irving's journey offers a compelling narrative of innovation, resilience, and the power of purpose-driven leadership.

Epilogue – Horizons of the Future from the Wings of Legacy and the Determination of the "Made Up Mind"

From the moment the first enslaved Africans were forced onto American soil, the journey toward freedom has been marked by resistance, resilience, and resolve. That same spirit, what we now call a "made up mind", echoes through every chapter of African American aviation history. It is the quiet force behind Bessie Coleman's decision to cross an ocean for flight training, Eugene Bullard's enlistment in a foreign army to earn his wings, and William J. Powell's rallying cry to "fill the skies with Black wings." These pioneers didn't wait for permission, they made up their minds to fly, and history followed.

John W. Greene Jr., Cornelius Coffey, and Willa Beatrice Brown transformed that resolve into institutions. They didn't just dream of flying, they built schools, trained mechanics, and opened airfields like Columbia Air Center, where the sky was no longer a ceiling but a gateway. Their minds were made up not only to fly but to teach others to fly, to repair, to lead. C. Alfred "Chief" Anderson's decision to train the Tuskegee Airmen wasn't just technical, it was revolutionary. His "made up mind" helped dismantle the myth of Black inferiority in combat aviation and proved that excellence knows no color.

The Tuskegee Airmen, led by Benjamin O. Davis Jr. and exemplified by Charles McGee, carried that same determination into war. Every mission flown, every bomber protected, every enemy aircraft downed was a declaration: We belong here! Their “made up minds” didn’t just win battles, they won dignity. And when Columbia Air Center rose from the fields of Croom, Maryland, it stood as a monument to self-determination. Pilots like Herbert Jones Jr. didn’t wait for access, they created it, proving that a “made up mind” can build airfields out of corn fields.

In the modern age, Barrington Irving’s solo flight around the world and his creation of the Flying Classroom shows that the legacy of resolve is alive and evolving. His mind was made up not only to fly but to educate, to inspire, and to lift others. General Charles Q. Brown Jr., Guion Bluford, and George London Jr. each carried that same internal fire to the highest levels of military and aerospace achievement. Their stories remind us that the cockpit is not just a place of flight, it’s a platform for transformation.

This book is not merely a chronicle of aviation; it is a testament to the power of a “made up mind”. Every figure within these pages faced exclusion, doubt, and danger, and every one of them chose to defy all that stood before them. Their legacy is not just in the aircraft they flew or the institutions they built, but in the unshakable decision to pursue flight against all odds. That decision, that “made up mind”, is the true engine of progress. And it is the inheritance of every reader who dares to dream beyond the horizon.

Author Stephen Ware standing next to Cessna N7615G. This aircraft was owned and operated by Herbert Jones Jr. of Cloud Club II, circa 2025.

About the Author

Stephen Christopher Ware has lived a life immersed in aviation. From his early days in the Civil Air Patrol to serving as an Aviation Support Equipment Electrician in the U.S. Navy, to his days of pilot training, and decades of professional work in the aerospace industry, the sky has always been his calling.

Beyond his career, Stephen has been a passionate student of aviation history. As a member of the Cloud Club II, he trained alongside pioneers and mentors who themselves carried forward the legacy of African American aviation. His personal journey brought him into contact with icons such as Colonel Charles McGee and Herbert Jones Jr., whose courage and mentorship inspired him to tell the story of resilience, determination, and achievement in African American aviation.

Married at the historic Columbia Air Center memorial, Stephen's life and work remain deeply focused on the history of not only African American aviation, but world aviation history. *Skybound* is both his tribute to the pioneers who opened the skies and his invitation for future generations of high-flying dreamers.

www.ingramcontent.com/pod-product-compliance
Lightning Source LLC
LaVergne TN
LVHW010841120826
845149LV00017B/3413

* 9 7 9 8 9 9 3 1 7 3 1 0 8 *